3/10

# WINTER OLYMPIC SPORTS

# SPEED SKATING

## by Joseph Gustaitis

Words that are defined in the glossary are in **bold** type the first time they appear in the text.

A table of abbreviations used for the names of countries appears on page 32.

**Crabtree editor**: Adrianna Morganelli
**Proofreader**: Crystal Sikkens
**Editorial director**: Kathy Middleton
**Production coordinator and
   prepress technician**: Katherine Berti
Developed for Crabtree Publishing Company by
RJF Publishing LLC (www.RJFpublishing.com)
**Editor**: Jacqueline Laks Gorman
**Designer**: Tammy West, Westgraphix LLC
**Photo Researcher**: Edward A. Thomas
**Indexer**: Nila Glikin

**Photo Credits**:
Corbis: Bettmann: p. 7, 8; Sergei Ilnitsky/epa: p. 28; Elizabeth
   Kreutz/NewSport: p. 12; Kim Kulish: p. 6
Getty Images: p. 5, 26; AFP: p. 2, 4, 9, 17, 18, 19, 20, 22, 27;
   Bongarts: p. 10; Sports Illustrated: p. 16
Landov: David Gray/Reuters: front cover, p. 24; Lee
   Jae-Won/Reuters: p. 23; Jerry Lampen/Reuters: p. 14
Wikipedia: Arnold C (Buchanan-Hermit): p. 29 (top);
   Thelastminute (Duncan Rawlinson): p. 29 (bottom)

**Cover**: Apolo Anton Ohno of the United States in the short
track speed skating competition at the 2006 Winter Olympics.

# CONTENTS

**Library and Archives Canada Cataloguing in Publication**

Gustaitis, Joseph Alan, 1944-
   Speed skating / Joseph Gustaitis.

(Winter Olympic sports)
Includes index.
ISBN 978-0-7787-4027-8 (bound).--ISBN 978-0-7787-4046-9 (pbk.)

   1. Speed skating--Juvenile literature. 2. Winter Olympics--
Juvenile literature. I. Title. II. Series: Winter Olympic sports

GV850.3.G88 2009          j796.91'4          C2009-903215-5

**Library of Congress Cataloging-in-Publication Data**

Gustaitis, Joseph Alan, 1944-
   Speed skating / Joseph Gustaitis.
      p. cm. --  (Winter Olympic sports)
   Includes index.

   ISBN 978-0-7787-4046-9 (pbk. : alk. paper)
-- ISBN 978-0-7787-4027-8 (reinforced library binding : alk. paper)
   1. Speed skating. I. Title.

GV850.3.G87 2010
796.91'4--dc22
                                                   2009021493

## Crabtree Publishing Company

www.crabtreebooks.com          1-800-387-7650
Copyright © **2010 CRABTREE PUBLISHING COMPANY**. All rights reserved. No part of this publication may be reproduced, stored in a retrieval
system or be transmitted in any form or by any means, electronic, mechanical, photocopying, recording, or otherwise, without the prior written permission
of Crabtree Publishing Company.

**Published in Canada**
**Crabtree Publishing**
616 Welland Ave.
St. Catharines, ON
L2M 5V6

**Published in the United States**
**Crabtree Publishing**
PMB16A
350 Fifth Ave., Suite 3308
New York, NY  10118

**Published in the United Kingdom**
**Crabtree Publishing**
White Cross Mills
High Town, Lancaster
LA1 4XS

**Published in Australia**
**Crabtree Publishing**
386 Mt. Alexander Rd.
Ascot Vale (Melbourne)
VIC 3032

# THE POWER OF SPEED

Speed skating is one of the most exciting sports at the Winter Olympics. The name explains why. It's all about *speed*. At the Olympics, there are two kinds of speed skating—long track and short track.

*Cindy Klassen (CAN), on track for a medal in 2006.*

## LONG TRACK

**Long track speed skating** is done on an oval ice rink that is 1,312 feet (400 meters) around. There are men's and women's races at 500m, 1,000m, 1,500m, and 5,000m. There is also a 3,000m race for women and a 10,000m race for men. Men and women also compete in a race called the **team pursuit**.

## SHORT TRACK

**Short track speed skating** is done on an oval track that is 364.57 feet (111.12 meters) around. The turns are tight and falls happen a lot. The men's and women's races are 500m, 1,000m, and 1,500m. There is also a 3,000m **relay** for women and a 5,000m relay for men.

## MOVING INSIDE

Speed skating used to take place outdoors. Since the 1990s, the Olympic races have taken place in special indoor ice rinks.

## OLD AND NEW

Long track speed skating began hundreds of years ago, in the 1200s. Short track speed skating is much newer. The sport did not begin until the early 1900s.

**OLYMPICS FACT FILE**

- The Olympic Games were first held in Olympia, in ancient Greece, around 3,000 years ago. They took place every four years until they were abolished in 393 A.D. A Frenchman named Pierre Coubertin (1863–1937) revived the Games, and the first modern Olympics — which featured only summer sports — were held in Athens in 1896.

- The first Olympic Winter Games were held in 1924 in Chamonix, France. The Winter Games were then held every four years except in 1940 and 1944 (because of World War II), taking place in the same year as the Summer Games, until 1992.

- The International Olympic Committee decided to stage the Summer and Winter Games in different years, so there was only a two-year gap before the next Winter Games were held in 1994. They have been held every four years from that time.

- The symbol of the Olympic Games is five interlocking colored rings. Together, they represent the union of the five regions of the world — Africa, the Americas, Asia, Europe, and Oceania (Australia and the Pacific Islands) — as athletes come together to compete in the Games.

# LONG TRACK SPEED SKATING

The Netherlands is a country with a lot of **canals**. During the Middle Ages, when the canals froze in winter, people used skates to travel on them. Then they started racing, and speed skating was born.

Dutch skaters Sven Kramer (left) and Carl Verheijen compete in the men's 5,000m at the 2006 Games.

## POPULARITY GROWS

After speed skating developed in the Netherlands, the sport became popular in other northern countries and spread to North America. When steel skates were invented in the United States around 1850, speed skating really took off.

## THAT'S FAST!

Speed skating is the fastest sport in the world that is human-powered and non-mechanical. Skaters can go faster than 37 MPH (60 km/h)!

## MEDAL WINNERS

In the first Winter Olympics, Clas Thunberg (FIN) won gold in the 1,500m and 5,000m. Since then, skaters from Northern Europe have continued to win. Norway has won the most medals in men's competition, while Germany and Russia have been the leaders in women's competition.

## WATCHING THE CLOCK

In long track, the skaters race, two at a time, against the clock. One skater starts on the inside lane, the other on the outside. Once every lap, the skaters change lanes. The skater with the fastest time wins.

*Speed skating at the 1932 Winter Olympic Games, when the competition was held outdoors.*

## SEE YOU AT THE OVAL

Long track at the Vancouver 2010 Olympics will be held at the Richmond Olympic Oval.

## CLAP SKATES AND OTHER GEAR

Starting with the 1998 Olympics, speed skaters began going faster because of a new skate called the clap skate. On older skates, the blade was attached to the boot at both ends. On a clap skate, the blade is attached, only at the front, with a **hinge** and spring. Skaters also wear skintight uniforms, pads, helmets, and sometimes goggles.

# MEN'S AND WOMEN'S 500M

**The 500m is over in about half a minute. You can't take your eyes off this race!**

*Catriona Le May Doan (CAN) celebrates her gold medal victory in the women's 500m in 2002.*

2006 OLYMPIC MEDALISTS: MEN:　　　GOLD: JOEY CHEEK (USA)
SILVER: DMITRY DOROFEEV (RUS)　　　BRONZE: LEE KANG-SEOK (KOR)

## DOING IT TWICE

Unlike the other long track events, the 500m is raced twice. Each racer begins one race in the inner lane and the other race in the outer lane. The two times are added together, and the fastest total time wins.

## THE OLYMPIC RECORD

Casey FitzRandolph (USA) set the men's Olympic record of 34.42 seconds in the 500m at the 2002 Olympics. It was only the second time he had won a 500m race in a major competition. Catriona Le May Doan (CAN) set the women's Olympic record of 37.30 seconds, also at the 2002 Olympics. She had also won the gold medal in 1998.

## A BUMP ON THE ICE

In the women's 500m race at the 1972 Olympics, 16-year-old Anne Henning (USA) was bumped by the other skater when changing lanes. That didn't stop Henning from setting an Olympic record. The rules said she could have another skate. She skated again and broke the record again. She also won the gold.

## AN OLYMPIC FAMILY

At the 1932 Olympics, Jack Shea (USA) won the 500m and the 1,500m in his hometown of Lake Placid, N.Y. Olympic competition ran in Shea's family. His son, Jim Shea, Sr., became a skier in the 1964 Winter Games— and his grandson, Jim Shea, Jr., won a gold medal in the skeleton competition in 2002. Three generations of a family had never competed in the Winter Olympics before.

*Anne Henning (USA) in action in 1972, setting a record in the women's 500m.*

# MEN'S AND WOMEN'S 1,000M AND 1,500M

Skaters in the 1,000m and the 1,500m need the kind of speed used in the 500m, but they also need **endurance**.

*Eric Heiden (USA) leads Gaétan Boucher (CAN) in the men's 1,000m in 1980, en route to winning five gold medals.*

2006 OLYMPIC MEDALISTS: MEN'S 1,000m:    GOLD: SHANI DAVIS (USA)
SILVER: JOEY CHEEK (USA)    BRONZE: ERBEN WENNEMARS (NED)
2006 OLYMPIC MEDALISTS: MEN'S 1,500m:    GOLD: ENRICO FABRIS (ITA)
SILVER: SHANI DAVIS (USA)    BRONZE: CHAD HEDRICK (USA)

The Olympic records in the men's and women's 1,000m and 1,500m races were all set at the 2002 Olympics. Among the men, Gerard van Velde (NED) holds the 1,000m record of 1:07.18, and Derek Para (USA) holds the 1,500m record of 1:43.95. Among the women, Chris Witty (USA) has the 1,000m record of 1:13.83, and Anni Friesinger (GER) has the 1,500m record of 1:54.02.

## DID YOU KNOW?

*The 1932 Games featured something that was never done again in the Olympics. Instead of having skaters race against the clock, two at a time, the 1932 speed skating events were held as actual races, involving five to six men in each **heat**. The top skaters in each heat moved on to skate in the next round of competition.*

## HARD LUCK KID

In the late 1980s, Dan Jansen (USA) was one of the world's best speed skaters. In the 1988 Games, however, he fell in two races and didn't win a medal. He didn't win a medal in the 1992 Games, either. In his first race at the 1994 Games, he lost his balance and finished eighth. In his last race — the 1,000m — he finally did it. He set a world record and won the gold medal.

## COMEBACK KID

Just 10 months before the 1984 Olympics, speed skater Gaétan Boucher (CAN) broke his ankle. It seemed that he would have to miss the Games. Not only did he get there, he won two gold medals — in the 1,000m and the 1,500m. By the time he retired after the 1988 Games, he also had a silver and a bronze.

## U.S. BEST

Bonnie Blair (USA) competed in the Winter Olympics in 1984, 1988, 1992, and 1994. She won five gold medals — the most by any U.S. woman in any sport — and a bronze. Her medals were all in the 500m and the 1,000m.

## TWO-SPORT CHAMPION

At the 1984 Winter Olympics, Christa Luding-Rothenburger (GDR) won the gold medal in the 500m. Four years later, she won the gold medal in the 1,000m and set a new world record. She wasn't done for the year. She went to the Summer Olympic Games and won a silver medal in cycling. She is the only person to win medals in both the Winter Olympics and the Summer Olympics in the same year.

**Dan Jansen (USA) after falling in 1988.**

| 2006 OLYMPIC MEDALISTS: WOMEN'S 1,000m: | GOLD: MARIANNE TIMMER (NED) |
|---|---|
| SILVER: CINDY KLASSEN (CAN) | BRONZE: ANNI FRIESINGER (GER) |
| 2006 OLYMPIC MEDALISTS: WOMEN'S 1,500m: | GOLD: CINDY KLASSEN (CAN) |
| SILVER: KRISTINA GROVES (CAN) | BRONZE: IREEN WÜST (NED) |

# WOMEN'S 3,000M

The 3,000m is considered a long race, but the skaters still go really fast—nearly 30 MPH (48 km/h)!

## DUTCH SURPRISE

Dutch skaters were not expected to do well in the women's 3,000m in 2006. Cindy Klassen (CAN), the world record holder, was in the race. So were two strong German skaters, Anni Friesinger and Claudia Pechstein. Ireen Wüst, a 19-year-old from the Netherlands, skated early in the race and finished in 4:02.43. She sat and waited while the other skaters tried to beat her time. No one did, and Wüst won the gold.

*Ireen Wüst (NED) skates to victory in the women's 3,000m race in 2006.*

## RECORD HOLDER

The Olympic record in the women's 3,000m race — 3:57.70 — belongs to Claudia Pechstein (GER), who set it in 2002. At the time of the race, Pechstein was the world record holder. She broke that record by more than 1 ½ seconds!

## THE FIRST AND ONLY

Lidiya Skoblikova (URS) won the women's 3,000m race at the 1964 Olympics. That was just one of four gold medals she won in speed skating at those Games. Four years before, Skoblikova had also won the 3,000m and the 1,500m at the Olympics. She was the first Winter athlete — man or woman — to win six gold medals in the Olympics. She is also the only woman in Winter Olympic history to win six golds in individual events.

## EIGHT IS ENOUGH

In the 3,000m women's race, Gunda Niemann-Stirnemann (GER) was one of the best. She won the gold medal in that race at the 1992 and 1998 Winter Olympics. In 1992, she also won the gold in the 5,000m. In all, she competed in four Olympics, winning eight medals (three gold, four silver, one bronze).

## TIE FOR SECOND

The women's 3,000m race at the 1964 Winter Games was won by Lidiya Skoblikova (URS) — the defending champion — with a time of 5:14.9. The silver medal was a surprise, though. The last athlete to compete was Han Pil-Hwa, an unknown skater from North Korea. She kept up with Skoblikova's pace for four of the seven laps, then could not keep it up. Han wound up in a tie for silver with Valentina Stenina (URS). No bronze medal was awarded that year.

## SILVER LINING

Andrea Ehrig (GDR) was an Olympic champion, with a gold medal in the 3,000m in 1984. She is best known, however, for all the silver medals she won — five, at three different Olympic Games. Ehrig — who also competed under the names of Andrea Mitscherlich and Andrea Schöne — captured her first silver in 1976 in the 3,000m, when she was just 15 years old. She did not medal in 1980, but took silver in 1984 in the 1,500m and 1,000m, in addition to her gold in the 3,000m. She closed out her career in 1988 with silver in the 3,000m and 5,000m and bronze in the 1,000m.

# MEN'S 5,000M

**Pace is important in a long race like the 5,000m.**

*Chad Hedrick (USA) celebrates his win in the 5,000m race at the 2006 Games.*

## KEEPING THE PACE

The 5,000m lasts a bit more than six minutes. Skaters like to keep the same speed during the whole race. If you see a skater slowing down, he's probably getting tired and isn't going to win.

## YOU CAN'T HAVE MY RECORD!

When Fred Maier (NOR) came to the 1968 Winter Olympics, he was the world record holder in the 5,000m. While he watched, Kees Verkerk (NED) broke Maier's record. No problem. Maier then went out and set the world record again. He also won the gold medal.

## SUPER STATS

Chad Hedrick (USA) won the 5,000m event in 2006 by a relatively wide margin (for speed skating). He put up a time of 6:14.68. The silver medalist, Sven Kramer (NED), skated the distance in 6:16.40, while the bronze medalist, Enrico Fabris (ITA), turned in a time of 6:18.25.

## DID YOU KNOW?

The first speed skater to represent his country at six consecutive Olympics never won a medal. Colin Coates (AUS) competed at the Olympics from 1968 through 1988, skating all the distances. His best result was a sixth place finish in the 10,000m in 1976.

## BEATING BAD LUCK

At the 1984 Olympics, Tomas Gustafson (SWE) won the gold medal in the 5,000m. After the Games, he had bad luck. His father died, he hurt his knee, and he had meningitis, a serious illness. He thought he might give up speed skating, but he didn't. He came back for the 1988 Games and won both the 5,000m and the 10,000m.

## DUTCH HERO

A year before the 1972 Winter Olympics, Ard Schenk (NED) set a world record in the 5,000m. In the Olympic race, though, there was no chance he would break that record. The competition was outdoors, and it was snowing. Even though he didn't break his record, Schenk still won easily. He also won two other gold medals. He was so popular in the Netherlands that a flower was named after him and he was featured on a postage stamp.

## ONE OF THE BEST

Johann Olav Koss (NOR) was one of the world's best speed skaters, but his Olympic experience started badly. In 1992, he was sick at the beginning of the Olympics and finished seventh in the 5,000m—and he was the world record holder at that distance. He recovered and won gold in the 1,500m and silver in the 10,000m. In 1996, he won gold in the 10,000m, 5,000m, and 1,500m. He donated the bonus money he was given by the Norwegian Athletic Federation to a charity to help children living in areas torn by war.

## RECORD SETTERS

Jochem Uytdehagge (NED) owns the Olympic record in the 5,000m— 6:14.66, set in 2002. The world record, however, belongs to Sven Kramer (NED), who skated the distance in 6:03.32 in November 2007.

## IN THE WAY

One of the competitors in the men's 5,000m race in 1948 lost a probable medal when a photographer got in his way on the final lap. Åke Seyffarth (SWE) had set a world record in the event years earlier. During the Olympics, though, he wound up seventh after brushing up against a photographer who had gone onto the ice. Seyffarth did win gold in the 10,000m and silver in the 1,500m.

*Canada's Clara Hughes (right), just before she overtook Claudia Pechstein (GER) for gold in the women's 5,000m.*

# WOMEN'S 5,000M

The 5,000m is the longest women's race. The skaters can't waste energy. They stand a little higher and try to go further with each stroke of the skate.

## THE FIRST WINNER

Two months before the 1988 Olympics, Yvonne van Gennip (NED) laced her skate too tightly and cut her foot. The cut got infected and she needed an operation. She still went to the Olympics and won three gold medals. Her third medal was in the 5,000m, which was being skated in the Olympics for the first time ever.

## DOMINATING PERFORMANCES

Claudia Pechstein (GER) competed in five Winter Olympics and won an amazing nine medals — more than any other speed skater in history! She won the gold in the 5,000m three times — in 1994, 1998, and 2002. In 1998, she set a world record when she won the race and beat her teammate, Gunda Niemann-Stirnemann, by just four-hundredths of a second.

## DON'T STAND UP STRAIGHT!

Good posture — standing up straight with the shoulders back — is not the preferred position for speed skaters. Instead, they skate with their knees and waist bent. They also lift their heads slightly so they can see the track. This position helps reduce **wind resistance**.

## DEFEATING THE CHAMPION

Clara Hughes (CAN) had already won a lot of races when she came to the Winter Olympics in 2006. One of the other skaters in the 5,000m, however, was the great Claudia Pechstein (GER). The race was 12 ½ laps, and Pechstein led for the first 10. Then Hughes put on a burst of speed. She passed Pechstein with just two laps left and won the gold medal.

## NOT TOO HOT, NOT TOO COLD

The temperature of the ice is important in speed skating. If the ice is too cold, the **friction** of the skate blade cannot create the thin layer of water that is necessary for proper skating. If the ice is too warm, too much water forms, which cuts down the skater's speed.

## RECORD SETTERS

Claudia Pechstein (GER) owns the Olympic record in the 5,000m — 6:46.91, set in 2002. The world record, however, belongs to Martina Sáblíková (CZE), who skated the distance in 6:45.61 in November 2007.

SILVER: CLAUDIA PECHSTEIN (GER)     BRONZE: CINDY KLASSEN (CAN)

# MEN'S 10,000M

The men's 10,000m is the longest Olympic speed skating race— and one of the most exhausting events.

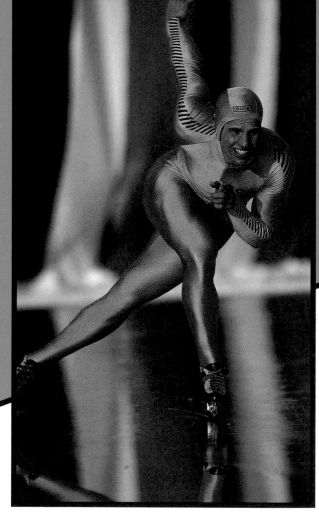

*Eric Heiden (USA), one of the best speed skaters in the history of the Olympic Games.*

## WHAT'S THE STRATEGY?

The 10,000m is almost 6¼ miles long and takes about 13 minutes. This race involves the most **strategy**. The most important thing is not to get too tired. Some skaters prefer to skate the first half of the race a little faster than the second half, but keeping a steady pace helps keep the skater from wearing out.

## AWESOME ERIC HEIDEN

On the morning of the 10,000m at the 1980 Olympics, Eric Heiden (USA) overslept. He hardly had time to eat breakfast and warm up, but it didn't matter. Heiden won the gold. He had already won gold medals in the 500m, 1,000m, 1,500m, and 5,000m—a total of five speed skating gold medals in one Olympics, setting records in every race! No one may ever **sweep** the races again. After he retired from competing, Heiden went to medical school and became an **orthopedic surgeon**. He was the team doctor for the U.S. speed skating team at the 2002 and 2006 Olympics.

## THE WIDEST MARGIN

Hjalmar Andersen (NOR) was the outstanding speed skater at the 1952 Winter Olympics. He won gold medals in the 1,500m, the 5,000m, and the 10,000m. When he won the 10,000m, he defeated the second-place skater by more than 24 seconds. No one since has won the Olympic 10,000m race by that much time.

*Jochem Uytdehaage of the Netherlands (center), after setting a world record in the 10,000m at the 2002 Games.*

# MEN'S AND WOMEN'S TEAM PURSUIT

The team pursuit is the newest Olympic long track event, first raced in 2006.

Team Italy, which won the men's team pursuit competition in 2006.

2006 OLYMPIC MEDALISTS: MEN:     GOLD: ITALY     SILVER: CANADA     BRONZE: NETHERLANDS

## ROUND AND ROUND THEY GO

In team pursuit, six skaters are on the ice at a time—two teams with three skaters each. The women's team pursuit is six laps long, and the men's is eight. Each skater takes a turn leading his or her team. The team's finishing time is when the last member crosses the finish line. There are **qualification rounds** during which teams are eliminated, leading up to the exciting final race.

## ITALIAN UPSET

Italy—a country that doesn't have a long history of speed skating success—upset the favorites to win the first Olympic gold medal in the men's team pursuit in 2006. The Italians beat Canada by more than two seconds. The Dutch were favored to win, but one of the team members crashed in a semifinal race and the team was eliminated.

The German women's team pursuit competitors in action in 2006.

## COMBINING THE RACES?

After the 2006 Olympics, the president of the **International Skating Union** (ISU) said that the men's and women's team pursuit might some day be combined into a single race, although not at the 2010 Olympics. The teams would have both men and women skaters.

## RECORD BUT NO GOLD

In 2006, Canada set the women's Olympic record in the team pursuit with a time of 3:01.24. The team, however, won only a silver medal because the record was set in a semifinal race, not the final race.

## EXPERIENCE COUNTS

At the 2006 Olympics, Germany won the gold medal in the women's race. The members of the team were very experienced. Although Daniela Anschütz-Thoms was in her first Olympics, Anni Friesinger was in her third and Claudia Pechstein was in her fifth.

# SHORT TRACK SPEED SKATING

Short track speed skating is fast and furious. The skaters crash into each other so often that the sport has been called **NASCAR** on ice!

Action during the men's 5,000m relay competition in short track speed skating at the 2006 Olympics.

## THE ROAD TO THE OLYMPICS

Short track began in the United States and Canada in the early 1900s. Short track became more and more popular, but the ISU didn't declare it an official sport until 1967. Short track did not become a regular Olympic event until 1992.

## RACING AGAINST EACH OTHER

In short track, there are four to six skaters in a race. The skaters race against each other—not against the clock. The first one across the finish line wins, and who goes the fastest doesn't always matter. There are a series of qualification rounds leading up to the final.

## MAKING THE TURNS

Because the track is only 364.57 feet (111.12 meters) around, short track skaters are almost always racing around a curve. They wear heavy skates that lace up high on the ankle, which helps them to stay steady around the turns. The blades don't run down the center of the boot but are off to one side. This also helps the skaters turn better.

## DISQUALIFIED!

There are many grounds for disqualification in short track speed skating. Among them are deliberately blocking, pushing, or getting in the way of another skater; slowing down unnecessarily; and purposely throwing oneself across the finish line. Skaters are also not allowed to conspire (work together) to affect the race's outcome.

## DID YOU KNOW?

South Korea has won the most Olympic medals in short track speed skating, with a total of 29 (17 gold, seven silver, and five bronze). Canada and China are tied for second with 20 short track medals apiece.

## VANCOUVER 2010

Short track at the Vancouver 2010 Olympics will be held at the Pacific Coliseum.

## AROUND AND AROUND

Since the track is so short, competitors have to skate a lot of laps! Here are the number of laps for each race:

- 500m — 4 ½ laps
- 1,000m — 9 laps
- 1,500m — 13 ½ laps
- 3,000m relay — 27 laps
- 5,000m relay — 45 laps

## DRESS FOR SUCCESS

Short track skaters need to wear helmets because of all the crashes. They also wear pads on their knees and shins so they won't get cut by other skaters' blades. They wear gloves to protect their hands from skate blades and because they often touch the ice while making turns. Finally, they wear special skintight suits to cut down wind resistance.

# MEN'S AND WOMEN'S 500M

The eventual medal winners fight for position during the women's 500m race in 2002.

**A skater has to get out to an early lead in the 500m—and try to stay there!**

**22** 2006 OLYMPIC MEDALISTS: MEN:        GOLD: APOLO ANTON OHNO (USA)
SILVER: FRANÇOIS-LOUIS TREMBLAY (CAN)        BRONZE: AHN HYUN-SOO (KOR)

## WHAT'S THE STRATEGY?

The skater wants to be either first or second at the first turn of the race, which is 4 ½ laps long. Skaters who are not in the lead watch to see if a skater in front of them makes a mistake. Then they try to pass.

## JUST PERFECT

Apolo Anton Ohno (USA) won the gold medal in the men's 500m in 2006 in what he called his "perfect race." He said he was in motion exactly when the **starting gun** went off. He took the lead early and found just the right path around the track. Ohno won in 41.935 seconds.

## THE FIRST WINNERS

The first woman to win the Olympic gold medal in the 500m was Cathy Turner (USA) in 1992. That year, there was no men's 500m in the Olympics. The first man to win gold was Chae Ji-Hoon (KOR) in 1994.

## DID YOU KNOW?

*Apolo Anton Ohno (USA), who has a total of five Olympic medals, won another award as well. In 2007, he appeared on the TV show* Dancing With the Stars *and ended up winning the competition.*

## SETTING THE RECORD

The Olympic record in the men's 500m short track race was set at the 2002 Games by Marc Gagnon (CAN), who won the gold with a blistering time of 41.802 seconds. Gagnon also won a bronze medal that year in the 1,500m race.

## WHICH YANG YANG?

The first Chinese athlete in history to win a gold medal at the Winter Olympics was Yang Yang, who won the women's 500m in 2002. There was, however, another woman on the Chinese short track team named Yang Yang, so the gold medal winner called herself Yang Yang (A). The "A" is for August, the month in which she was born.

*Apolo Anton Ohno (USA) crosses the finish line, winning the men's 500m in 2006.*

2006 OLYMPIC MEDALISTS: WOMEN:   GOLD: WANG MENG (CHN)
SILVER: EVGENIA RADANOVA (BUL)   BRONZE: ANOUK LEBLANC-BOUCHER (CAN)

# MEN'S AND WOMEN'S 1,000M AND 1,500M

In these races you have to be fast—and smart!
You have to pass at just the right time.

*Steven Bradbury (AUS), winning the men's 1,000m in 2002 when everyone else fell down.*

| | |
|---|---|
| 2006 OLYMPIC MEDALISTS:  MEN'S 1,000m: | GOLD: AHN HYUN-SOO (KOR) |
| SILVER: LEE HO-SUK (KOR) | BRONZE: APOLO ANTON OHNO (USA) |
| 2006 OLYMPIC MEDALISTS:  MEN'S 1,500m: | GOLD: AHN HYUN-SOO (KOR) |
| SILVER: LEE HO-SUK (KOR) | BRONZE: LI JIAJUN (CHN) |

## SUPER STATS

Yang Yang (A) (CHN) holds the Olympic record in the women's 1,000m of 1:31.235, set in 2002. The men's 1,000m record, set in 2006, is held by Ahn Hyun-Soo (KOR) — 1:26.739. The women's 1,500m record, 2:21.069, is held by Choi Eun-Kyung (KOR), who set it in 2002. The men's 1,500m record, 2:15.942, is held by Kim Dong-Sung (KOR). He also set it in 2002.

## DID YOU KNOW?

*It is important that a short track speed skater not get injured during the Olympics. If a competitor qualifies for the final in an event and becomes hurt before she can race, she can't be replaced. Such injuries are possible since there are often several days between the first rounds and the final of short track skating events.*

## STRATEGY COUNTS

The longer short track races have been called "cat and mouse" races. The first half of the races can be slow, as skaters wait for the right time to move. As the end gets near, some skaters like to stay in second place and then try to pass the leader at just the right moment.

## TALK ABOUT LUCK!

The men's 1,000m at the 2002 Olympics had an unlikely winner. In the finals of the event, Steven Bradbury (AUS) — who barely made it to the final round — was in last place. Then there was a crash and the four other skaters fell. Bradbury skated past them all and won the gold medal. He became the first athlete from the Southern Hemisphere to win gold at the Winter Olympics.

## CUTTING IT LOOSE

When Chun Lee-Kyung (KOR) won the gold medal in the women's 1,000m in 1994, she beat Nathalie Lambert (CAN) by just one-tenth of a second.

## KOREAN POWER

Skaters from South Korea have made short track their specialty. At the 2006 Games, Ahn Hyun-Soo won gold medals in the men's 1,000m and 1,500m. Jin Sun-Yu also won two gold medals — in the women's 1,000m and 1,500m.

## YOUNGEST WINNER

At the 2002 Olympics, Ko Gi-Hyun (KOR) won the gold medal in the women's 1,500m. She was only 15! She was the youngest winner ever in short track at the Olympics. Choi Eun-Kyung, who was on the same team, set a world record in the semifinals, but Ko beat her in the final.

2006 OLYMPIC MEDALISTS: WOMEN'S 1,000m: GOLD: JIN SUN-YU (KOR)
SILVER: WANG MENG (CHN) BRONZE: YANG YANG (A) (CHN)
2006 OLYMPIC MEDALISTS: WOMEN'S 1,500m: GOLD: JIN SUN-YU (KOR)
SILVER: CHOI EUN-KYUNG (KOR) BRONZE: WANG MENG (CHN)

# SHORT TRACK RELAYS

With so many skaters on the ice, the relays are both dangerous and dizzying.

*Skaters in action during the exciting men's 5,000m relay in 2006.*

2006 OLYMPIC MEDALISTS: MEN:     GOLD: SOUTH KOREA
                                  SILVER: CANADA          BRONZE: UNITED STATES

## SUPER STATS

South Korean women have won four of the five gold medals ever awarded in the relay — in 1994, 1998, 2002, and 2006.

## DID YOU KNOW?

The women's short track relay is 3,000m long, while the men's is 5,000m.

## RELAY FORMAT

The short track relays take place over two days. Eight teams of men and eight teams of women are divided into two groups that race against each other. The top four men's and women's teams advance to the finals.

## CROWD CONTROL

Relay teams have four skaters each, so if four teams are racing, there are 16 skaters on the track. The ice is really crowded! One skater from each team starts the race while her teammates wait in the center of the track. When a skater comes out from the center to begin skating, the skater on the ice gives her a push on the back.

## THE OLYMPIC RECORD

The Olympic record in the men's relay — 6:43.376 — was set in 2006 by the team from South Korea. One member, Ahn Hyun-Soo, also won two gold medals in individual races. Another member, Lee Ho-Suk, won two silvers. No wonder they were so good!

## DANGER!

Crashes in the relay can be serious. In one race at the 2002 Olympics, a collision on the 17th lap sent two skaters falling to the ice. Min Ryoung (KOR) slid across the ice and crashed into the wall. He was carried out on a stretcher and sent to the hospital. The next day, he dropped out of the Games.

*The South Korean team maneuvers for position during the men's 5,000m relay.*

# A SNAPSHOT OF THE VANCOUVER 2010 WINTER OLYMPICS

## SPEED SKATING
## THE ATHLETES

Everyone is getting ready for Vancouver in 2010! Olympic teams are still being determined. The listings below include the top finishers in a selection of events in the 2008-2009 World Cup. Who among them will be the athletes to watch in the Vancouver Winter Olympics? Visit the Web site www.vancouver2010.com for more information about the upcoming competitions.

*Shani Davis of the USA in action during the men's 1000m competition at the World Sprint Speed Skating Championships in Moscow, Russia, January 2009. Shani Davis won the gold medal and becomes overall champion at the World Sprint Speed Skating Championships.*

## SPEED SKATING EVENTS

**Men — 100m:**
1. Yuya Oikawa (JPN)
2. Yu Fengtong (CHN)
3. Lee Kang-seok (KOR)

**Men — 1500m:**
1. Shani Davis (USA)
2. Trevor Marsicano (USA)
3. Havard Bokko (NOR)

**Men — Team pursuit:**
1. Canada
2. Italy
3. Japan

**Women — 100m:**
1. Jenny Wolf (GER)
2. Thijsje Oenema (NED)
3. Aihua Xing (CHN)

**Women — 1500m:**
1. Kristina Groves (CAN)
2. Daniela Anschutz (GER)
3. Christine Nesbitt (CAN)

**Women — Team pursuit:**
1. Czech Republic
2. USA
3. Netherlands

# THE VENUES IN VANCOUVER

# PACIFIC COLISEUM

# RICHMOND OLYMPIC OVAL

- **venue capacity: 14,239**
- **located in Vancouver, British Columbia**
- **elevation: 85 feet (26 m)**

- **venue capacity: 8000**
- **located in Richmond, British Columbia on the banks of the Fraser River**
- **elevation: sea level**

*Pacific Coliseum*

*Richmond Olympic Oval*

# GLOSSARY

**canal** A man-made waterway that is dug across land

**disqualified** To be eliminated from competition for not following the rules

**endurance** The ability to keep at a difficult activity for a long time

**friction** Resistance met by a moving object

**heat** One run down a course in a competition

**hinge** A movable joint that makes it possible for something to bend one way, then bend back into position

**International Skating Union (ISU)** The international governing body of both figure skating and speed skating

**long track speed skating** A type of speed skating, done on an oval 1,312 feet (400 meters) around, that has been in the Olympics since 1924

**NASCAR** The National Association for Stock Car Auto Racing, which sponsors stock car races in the United States

**orthopedic surgeon** A doctor who specializes in the treatment of the skeletal system, or bones

**qualification round** A stage of competition that competitors must succeed at in order to move on to the next stage

**relay** A type of race in which teams compete, with each member of the team going part of the distance

**short track speed skating** A type of speed skating, done on a track that is 364.57 feet (111.12 meters) around, that has been in the Olympics since 1992

**starting gun** A type of pistol that is used in races to let the racers know when to begin

**strategy** A careful plan of action used to achieve a goal

**sweep** To win all the prizes or events in a competition

**team pursuit** A type of long track speed skating that has two teams with three skaters each on the ice at a time

**wind resistance** A force created by air that resists the movement of something that is going forward

# FIND OUT MORE

## BOOKS

Bourassa, Barbara. *Winter Sports* (North Mankato, MN: QEB Publishing, 2007)

Hughes, Morgan. *Ice Skating* (Vero Beach, FL: Rourke Publishing, 2005)

Judd, Ron C. *The Winter Olympics: An Insider's Guide to the Legends, the Lore, and the Games* (Seattle: Mountaineers Books, 2009)

Marsico, Katie, and Cecilia Minden. *Speed Skating* (Ann Arbor, MI: Cherry Lake Publishing, 2008)

U.S. Olympic Committee, *A Basic Guide to Speed Skating* (Santa Ana, CA: Griffin Publishing, 2002)

## WEB SITES

**International Olympic Committee    www.olympic.org**
The official site of the International Olympic Committee, with information on all Olympic sports.

**International Skating Union        www.isu.org**
The official site of the world governing body of skating.

**Speed Skating                     www.nbcolympics.com/speedskating/index.html**
From NBC Television, a site that recaps speed skating at the 2006 Olympics and previews the 2010 Olympics, while also providing good information about the sport.

**Speed Skating Canada              www.speedskating.ca**
The official site of Speed Skating Canada, with news on Canadian and international competitions and good information on the sport.

**U.S. Olympic Committee            www.usoc.org/**
The official site of the U.S. Olympic Committee, with information on athletes, sports, and the Olympics.

**US Speedskating                   www.usspeedskating.org**
The official site of the national governing group for speed skating in the United States.

## COUNTRY ABBREVIATIONS

AUS — Australia
BUL — Bulgaria
CAN — Canada
CHN — China
CZE — Czech Republic
FIN — Finland
GDR — East Germany (1949–1990)
GER — Germany
ITA — Italy
KOR — South Korea
NED — Netherlands
NOR — Norway
RUS — Russia
SWE — Sweden
URS — Soviet Union (1922–1992)
USA — United States of America

Printed in the U.S.A. — CG